Gluten free *diet*

igloobooks

Published in 2016
by Igloo Books Ltd
Cottage Farm
Sywell
NN6 0BJ
www.igloobooks.com

Cover images: Main Thinkstock / Getty; all other images Photocuisine UK

LEO002 0316
4 6 8 10 9 7 5 3
ISBN 978-1-78440-687-5

Printed and manufactured in China

Contents

Gluten-free champion

The tennis player Novak Djokovic does not have coeliac disease (see page 8), but he believes that an intolerance to gluten led to a lack of energy, and symptoms similar to asthma. In 2011, he cut out gluten from his diet entirely and the results were staggering. He says that he felt quicker and lighter, and had lots more energy. Since changing his diet, he has consistently been ranked no lower than number two in the world.

Introduction

Sometimes it seems like every week there's another story in the news about a food that we should avoid. First it was fat and cholesterol, then carbs, then sugar and alcohol. Now there's a lot of talk about going gluten-free. Celebrities are doing it, and most supermarkets now have a well-stocked gluten-free section. But, what exactly is gluten, and why are so many people trying to avoid it?

What is gluten?

In simple terms, gluten is a general name for the proteins found in wheat and some other grains. Its name comes from the Latin word for 'glue' and it is what makes pastry puffy and pizza dough stretchy. It can be found in wheat, barley, rye, most oats and the foods that contain them – such as bread, pasta, beer and cereals. For a few people, eating gluten can cause serious health problems, but for most people, eating it has no adverse effects.

Healthy living

Many people who have gone gluten-free are quick to sing its praises. Eliminating gluten has helped them lose weight, they say, as well as giving them more energy and a clearer mind. Going gluten-free can be tricky, since it is found in so many popular foods. But for some people, it's worth the trouble. Could gluten-free be the right diet for you?

Why Go Gluten-free?

Some people have no choice about going gluten-free. They may suffer from coeliac disease, a lifelong autoimmune disorder. A coeliac sufferer's immune system reacts to gluten by attacking the lining of the small intestine. Over time, this damage can leave the small intestine unable to efficiently absorb nutrients from food, leaving the person malnourished.

For somebody with coeliac disease, eating gluten may cause symptoms including bloating, diarrhoea, nausea, fatigue, headaches and weight loss. Over the long term, it may lead to osteoporosis and anaemia, as well as some cancers. There is no cure for coeliac disease, but switching to a strict gluten-free diet will eliminate the symptoms and avoid damage to the small intestine.

Gluten sensitivity

Some people who do not have coeliac disease are still affected by eating gluten – this is called non-coeliac gluten sensitivity. It is still not completely understood by scientists. The symptoms are mostly the same as for a coeliac disease sufferer, but no damage occurs to the small intestine if gluten is eaten. This condition is currently being researched and there is no specific test to diagnose it. However, many people who have tested negative for coeliac disease see an improvement in their gut symptoms after cutting out gluten from their diet.

Wheat allergy

Some people are allergic to wheat. When they eat it, their immune system reacts by producing antibodies. These can cause symptoms such as watery eyes, itching, rashes, coughing, breathing difficulties, headaches and nausea. A wheat allergy can be diagnosed by a doctor by carrying out a skin-prick test. Foods labelled 'gluten-free' are not always safe for people with wheat allergies, as the food may still contain wheat, even though the gluten has been removed.

Making a choice

Coeliac disease probably affects about one in 100 people, though many of these people are undiagnosed. Wheat allergy affects even fewer – mainly children will outgrow it by the time they reach adulthood. There are no reliable statistics for people with non-coeliac gluten sensitivity. Even so, that leaves a fairly small slice of the population with a medical reason to avoid gluten. So why are so many otherwise healthy people going gluten-free?

Is it healthier?

There is a perception that going gluten-free is a healthier way of living. Celebrities and sports stars who have given up gluten are a great advertisement for this – they are successful, and they look fabulous! With the range of gluten-free foods that are now available, it has never been easier to give it a try. But so far, scientists have not found evidence that gluten is harmful or fattening, except for the minority of people with a sensitivity or allergy.

Out with the bad...

One compelling reason to give up gluten is that it often leads to a healthier diet overall. Many foods that contain gluten, such as cakes and biscuits, are unhealthy in other ways – high in fat and sugar, for example. Going gluten-free means taking a long, hard look at your diet to see where changes can be made. Often you end up replacing gluten-containing foods with healthier alternatives, such as lean proteins and vegetables, which can only be a good thing!

Gluten and carbs

Many popular diets are focused around reducing carbohydrate intake, especially so-called 'empty carbs', such as those found in white bread, sugar, white rice, cakes and biscuits. A lot of people are able to lose weight by replacing these foods in their diet with whole grains, vegetables and lean meats. Many of the foods that contain gluten are also high in carbohydrates, so eliminating them may help you lose weight.

Before You Start

If you're planning to go gluten-free because you want a healthier diet overall, great! But if you think you may have coeliac disease or a wheat allergy, it's important to get a proper diagnosis from a doctor. Here is a list of symptoms that may indicate coeliac disease:

- persistent diarrhoea, constipation or wind
- nausea and vomiting

- cramping or bloating
- tiredness and headaches
- unexplained weight loss
- skin rash
- numbness and tingling in the hands and feet.

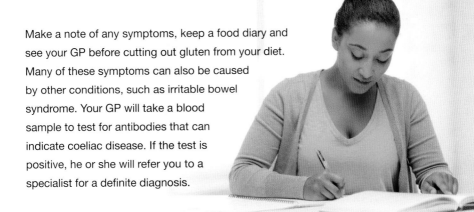

Make a note of any symptoms, keep a food diary and see your GP before cutting out gluten from your diet. Many of these symptoms can also be caused by other conditions, such as irritable bowel syndrome. Your GP will take a blood sample to test for antibodies that can indicate coeliac disease. If the test is positive, he or she will refer you to a specialist for a definite diagnosis.

A helping hand

It is important to know if you have coeliac disease and once you're diagnosed your GP will be able to offer support, including referrals to specialist dietitians. The only treatment for coeliac disease is to go gluten-free permanently. This can be a difficult adjustment, but a dietitian will be able to help.

Stay safe

Even if you don't think you have coeliac disease or a wheat allergy, it is always a good idea to talk to your GP before starting a new diet. They will be able to offer advice on the safest and healthiest way to lose weight, and they can provide information about achieving a more balanced diet.

Getting support

If you are diagnosed with coeliac disease, you shouldn't feel alone. There are numerous organisations and charities focused on helping people with the condition. Your GP can put you in touch with people that can offer information, advice and support.

A Balanced Diet

No matter what diet you choose to follow, it's important to give your body the right balance of nutrients. Your body doesn't actually need gluten, so there are no harmful effects as a result of giving it up. However, many of the foods that contain gluten also contain other vital nutrients, such as fibre, iron, folic acid and B vitamins. If you are cutting gluten-based foods out of your diet, you will need to find another source of these important nutrients.

As with any diet, the key is to eat a balance of different types of food. For example, everyone should eat at least five portions of fruit and vegetables each day and this won't change on a gluten-free diet. Fruit and vegetables are naturally gluten-free and they are packed with vitamins and minerals. For sources of protein, stick to pulses, nuts, leafy greens, lean meats and fish. Try to keep salt, sugar and fat to a minimum.

Grains and starches

Grains and starchy foods are usually the trickiest part of a gluten-free diet. Cutting out wheat eliminates a big category of foods from your diet, but there are others to replace them. You can replace wheat, rye and barley with rice, potatoes, sweet potatoes and a variety of naturally gluten-free grains. You can also buy gluten-free versions of many common foods, such as bread, cereal and pasta.

Fibre

On a gluten-free diet, you need to make sure that you get enough fibre. Fibre passes through the body without being absorbed, and it is found in many wholegrain cereals, including wheat. Cutting out wheat, rye and barley may mean you are no longer getting enough fibre. Foods such as brown rice, corn, peas, beans and lentils are all good sources of fibre. Try to include these foods in your gluten-free diet.

What to Eat

If you make a list of all the different foods you eat that contain wheat, the thought of cutting them out may seem impossible. But there are a lot of delicious substitutes for these foods, and most of them have become more easily available in the last decade. 'Gluten-free' doesn't have to mean 'grain-free'!

What grains can I eat?

On this diet you can safely eat brown rice and sweetcorn (even popcorn!), as well as quinoa, buckwheat, millet, sorghum and amaranth. Oats are naturally gluten-free as well, but they are nearly always contaminated with gluten during processing, so make sure you choose those that are marked as 'gluten-free'. These grains are a good source of energy, and they also provide iron, calcium, fibre and B vitamins. If you've never cooked with these grains before, don't panic – this book has recipes that will show you exactly what to do!

Making changes

The great thing about going gluten-free is that it doesn't necessarily mean you have to eat less, just differently. By replacing refined foods, such as white bread, with healthier alternatives, you'll be doing your body a lot of good. Focusing on whole foods, such as lean meats, fish, vegetables and whole grains, is the foundation of a healthy diet.

Iron

Iron is important in any diet, but even more so for people with coeliac disease. Damage to the small intestine can mean that the body doesn't absorb iron very well, leaving them anaemic. Even if you don't have coeliac disease, you need to watch your iron intake. Wheat flour is usually enriched with iron, but gluten-free flours aren't. To make sure you are getting enough iron, eat red meat, liver, leafy green vegetables, pulses, dried fruits, nuts and seeds.

Which foods contain gluten?

It's obvious that some foods contain gluten – bagels, for example, or croissants – but a lot of gluten is 'hiding' in places where you might not expect to find it, such as in packaged sauces or dressings. When in doubt, always check the label.

In addition to bread and pasta, you'll need to avoid couscous, flour tortillas, most noodles, muffins, pastries, many breakfast cereals, biscuits (sweet and savoury) and cakes. These are all usually made with wheat, although gluten-free versions are available. You'll also need to cut out a whole list of other foods that contain gluten: beer, some gravy, many salad dressings, breadcrumbs and croutons, anything cooked in batter, and barley water to name just a few.

Gluten-free on a budget

Gluten-free products, such as bread, may save time, but they can also cost three or four times as much as the wheat-based version. However, going gluten-free doesn't have to break the bank! By cooking as much as possible yourself, you'll save money and have the confidence that comes from knowing exactly what you're eating. You can make big batches of soup, chilli or curry and freeze individual portions for when you're in a hurry.

Hidden gluten

Processed foods often contain gluten because food manufacturers use it as an additive. Gluten can be added to foods to stabilise or thicken them and to keep them from separating. Be especially wary of tinned meat products, condiments, pasta sauces, barbecue sauces, soy sauce, processed meats, stock and anything containing gravy.

Reading Food Labels

To go gluten-free, you'll have to become an expert at reading food labels. Gluten can be part of nearly every food, but it's not always easy to spot on the label. Some foods are designed to be gluten-free, and they will have a prominent label saying so. Some foods display the 'crossed grain' symbol developed by the charity Coeliac UK, which shows that a product is certified gluten-free.

What to look for

There are strict laws controlling the way that food is labelled. Only foods that contain less than 20 parts per million of gluten can be labelled 'gluten-free'. These include flour substitute products, such as breads and crackers, as well as processed foods that are naturally gluten-free, like soups and crisps.

Other labels

There is another category, 'very low gluten', for substitute products containing between 20 and 100 parts per million, although this is very rare. Some foods may carry a label stating 'no gluten-containing ingredients'. The use of this term isn't covered by the law, but it is used by manufacturers and caterers to identify foods that are made with ingredients that don't contain gluten, where they are confident that there has been no cross contamination.

Cross contamination

Any time that a gluten-free food comes into contact with gluten, it is called cross contamination. This can happen at nearly any point from farm to plate: during harvesting, transport, processing, cooking and serving. Cross contamination is common in factories where many different food types are processed, and this is why people with coeliac disease avoid eating regular oats. Cross contamination can even be a problem at home if you don't properly clean your pans, utensils and chopping boards after preparing foods with gluten.

If a product is clearly labelled 'gluten-free', it makes life much easier! The use of this term is strictly regulated, so you can be confident that these products are safe. On products without this label, you have to look very carefully to find the gluten listed. If a product uses a gluten-containing cereal as an ingredient, it must be listed in the ingredients list, no matter how little of it is used. These include wheat, barley, rye, oats, spelt and khorasan wheat (sometimes called Kamut®).

Hidden gluten

So far, so simple. But there are also a host of other ingredients that are derived from gluten-containing cereals. Keep your eyes peeled for terms such as malt extract and brewer's yeast. To make things even trickier, there are many different varieties of wheat: bulgar and durum are just two of them.

Gluten-free but fattening

Don't forget to check the other nutritional information as well, including sugar, salt and fat content. Foods that are specifically designed to be gluten-free often have extra sugar and fat added to make up for the missing gluten. Why not try making your own gluten-free bread or bagels? With the right recipe, it's not difficult and you'll save money.

New rules

New laws came into place in 2014 that affect the labelling of food. Any food considered to be an allergen (which includes gluten-containing ingredients) must now be emphasised in the ingredients list. They might be in italics, underlined or in bold type – anything that makes them stand out. This will make it easier to identify products containing gluten.

Eating Out

Having a meal out is a fantastic treat, but it can be tricky if you are on a gluten-free diet. Luckily, in the past few years, restaurants have become much more aware of people's need for gluten-free food. Many menus list any dishes that are gluten-free, and kitchen staff are often more informed about how to avoid cross contamination during food preparation.

Plan ahead

If you're worried, check out the restaurant's website before you go. Many chain restaurants have allergy information on their websites. You could also call and speak to someone before you go. By talking to staff about their procedures, you can gauge their level of awareness. For example, if they list their chips as gluten-free, ask them if the oil used for chips is also used to fry battered foods – the flour or breadcrumbs contaminate the oil.

Here are a few tips for enjoying your meal with confidence:

- Arrive with a positive mindset, getting excited about what you can eat, rather than focusing on what you can't.

- Tell your server that you are on a gluten-free diet. He or she may be able to make suggestions of suitable dishes. So many people are eating gluten-free that they will be used to being asked about the menu options!

- Stick to foods that are naturally gluten-free, such as potatoes, rice, meat, fish and vegetables.

- Don't be afraid to order your food exactly as you want it. Sauces and salad dressings are often hidden sources of gluten. If in any doubt, ask to have it without.

- Some food types, such as Indian and Thai, are usually made with mainly gluten-free ingredients, so these can be good options. Always check the ingredients with your server to make sure.

Losing Weight

Some people have no choice about going gluten-free, but many others adopt the diet in order to lose weight and feel healthier. The truth is that unless you suffer from coeliac disease, a wheat allergy or gluten sensitivity, there is no evidence that eating gluten is harmful or fattening. However, many people do lose weight and look fabulous on a gluten-free diet. How do they do it?

Cutting out the bad

Many of us eat a diet that relies heavily on wheat-based products. This is not necessarily a bad thing – after all, whole grains are an important source of fibre and other nutrients. But there are a lot of wheat-based foods that are less healthy. Biscuits, cakes and pastries are obvious examples of this, but what about that slice of lovely wholegrain bread you had for breakfast, slathered with fatty butter and sugary jam? Or the floury batter on your deep-fried fish and chips?

Changing diet

By cutting out wheat, many people find that their whole diet changes. It's not about replacing their normal food with like-for-like gluten-free substitutes, which are often high in fat or sugar, and nearly always more expensive. Instead, they switch to grains such as brown rice, which pack a big nutritional punch while containing relatively few calories. They eat more vegetables and pulses and pay close attention to exactly what they're eating. This balanced approach can make you healthier overall and help you lose weight.

The big picture

Just because a food is gluten-free doesn't necessarily mean that it is healthy. After all, a gluten-free cake is still a cake! You need to look at all the nutritional content of a food before choosing it: fat, sugar, fibre, carbohydrates, vitamins and more.

Being Active, Staying Safe

Going gluten-free is a great start, but any plan to lose weight must be more than just a new food regime. You need to stay active, to burn off calories as well as improve your overall health. If you reduce your fat and sugar intake as part of your gluten-free diet, you'll probably lose weight, and if you increase the amount of exercise you do then you'll lose even more!

Keep it simple

Many people are reluctant to start an exercise programme because they think they need to join the gym or get a new workout wardrobe. Remember that you don't need to break a sweat to get the benefit from exercise. If you keep moving throughout the day, you'll get just as much benefit as you would from a 30-minute jog. Take the stairs whenever you can, park at the far end of the supermarket car park or get off the bus two or three stops earlier than usual. Over the course of a day, these little bits of exercise can add up!

The more the merrier

One of the most effective things you can do is to find a friend who's also trying to become more active. Having a friend to exercise with can keep you motivated, and you're more likely to stick with it. It doesn't have to be a competition to see who can run for longer or do more crunches – instead, it can be a great opportunity for a chat!

Side benefits

Keeping active is not just about losing weight! Regular exercise will strengthen muscles and bones, keep your heart healthy and reduce your risk of serious illnesses, such as diabetes or stroke. And although it might sound crazy, regular exercise can also make you feel more energetic.

Warming up

Make sure that your body is ready before exercising. You need to gently stretch and warm up your muscles before an exercise session to reduce the risk of injury. Stretching can also improve your overall flexibility and muscle tone. Once you've finished exercising, some deep breathing, accompanied by more stretching, is a great way to cool down.

Step it up

Once you get into the swing of things with your new diet, you may feel like you have more energy. Well, now is the time to use it! Swimming is a fantastic way to burn calories. It's non-weight-bearing, so it puts less pressure on your joints. Walking, jogging and cycling are also great ways to burn calories while you're enjoying the fresh air and exploring your town, city or countryside. If the weather's bad and you're stuck indoors, you can burn calories doing the housework.

A family affair

If you have children, get them exercising with you! Take them to the park, but instead of sitting on a bench texting while they play, join in for some football, tag or hide and seek. If you have a dog, make a point of taking it for a walk or jog every day. If you don't, why not borrow one? You might be able to help an elderly neighbour who can't give their pet the exercise it needs.

Stay safe

If you're new to exercising, or you have any specific health conditions, it's best to talk to your GP, gym instructor or personal trainer before you start a fitness programme. They'll be able to offer support and advice on the best and safest ways to keep fit and lose weight.

Keeping Motivated

Sticking to a gluten-free diet can be hard work, so it's important to stay motivated. First and foremost, you need to have a clear idea of why you're doing it and what you expect to get out of it. Why not write a list of your reasons for going gluten-free? Keep it handy, so you can remind yourself if you ever get tempted to 'cheat'.

Setting goals

Many people who go gluten-free do it in order to feel better and to lose weight. What are your goals? Think about what you can achieve in the short term, as well as the long term. If you have a target weight or dress size, write it down and make a plan for achieving it.

Before you begin the new diet, start a diary that lists what you eat and do each day, as well as how you feel. After a few weeks, go back and read the earliest entries. You'll probably find that your energy levels and health have improved, even if you didn't realise it at the time.

Reward yourself

Star charts work for children, so why not try it yourself? Every day that you stick to the gluten-free diet or achieve your exercise targets, give yourself a star. Once you've earned enough stars, you can reward yourself.

Tell your friends

You're not in this alone. Make sure that your friends and family know about your gluten-free diet. If they know what you're doing, they can offer help and support, and they'll know not to tempt you with foods that you can no longer eat. They might want to join you for a jog, or even try cooking gluten-free foods with you!

Breakfast and Brunch

If you're used to starting your day with toast or cereal, breakfast can be one of the trickiest meals on a gluten-free diet. Supermarket shelves are full of gluten-free substitutes for bread, muffins and breakfast cereals, but these gluten-free products are often no healthier than the original version. Now is your chance to make a change!

Porridge made from gluten-free oats is a great start to the day, as it will give you slow-burning energy that will take you all the way to lunch. Or try a yoghurt with fresh berries and gluten-free muesli.

If you really can't give up your morning toast, use gluten-free wholegrain bread and spread, such as soft cheese or mashed avocado. These provide nutrients without the sugar found in jam and other breakfast spreads.

Buckwheat Waffles

Serves: 6–8
Preparation time: 10 minutes
Cooking time: 15–20 minutes
Calories/serving: 350–262

Ingredients

300 g / 10 ½ oz / 2 cups buckwheat flour

1 tbsp gluten-free baking powder

1 tbsp caster (superfine) sugar

½ tsp salt

2 large eggs, beaten

375 ml / 13 fl. oz / 1 ½ cups
semi-skimmed milk

75 g / 3 oz / ⅓ cup unsalted butter, melted

½ tsp vanilla extract

1 tbsp sunflower oil, for greasing

1 tbsp icing (confectioners') sugar, to dust

Method

1. Mix the flour, baking powder, sugar and salt in a large mixing bowl and then beat together the eggs, milk, melted butter and vanilla extract in a measuring jug.

2. Slowly add to the dry ingredients, whisking at the same time until you have a smooth batter.

3. Preheat a waffle iron and wipe the surface with a little sunflower oil.

4. Ladle the batter into the iron and close; cook according to manufacturer's instructions until the waffles are golden and set.

5. Repeat this method to cook the remaining batter until you have used all of it.

6. Dust lightly with icing sugar before serving.

Summer Fruit Porridge

Serves: 4
Preparation time: 10–15 minutes
Cooking time: 10 minutes
Calories/serving: 237

Ingredients

150 g / 5 oz / 1 cup raspberries

110 g / 4 oz / ⅔ cup strawberries,
   hulled and chopped

1 tbsp caster (superfine) sugar

½ lemon, juiced

150 g / 5 oz / 1 ½ cups gluten-free rolled oats

150 ml / 5 fl. oz / ⅔ cup cold water

150 ml / 5 fl. oz / ⅔ cup semi-skimmed milk

Method

1. Combine the raspberries, strawberries, sugar and lemon juice in a mixing bowl. Stir well and cover, then set to one side for 10 minutes.

2. Combine the oats, water and milk in a medium saucepan set over a medium heat.

3. Cook, stirring frequently, until the oats start to absorb the liquid and swell; the porridge should be thick and creamy in consistency.

4. Spoon it into serving bowls before stirring through the fruit and any accumulated juices.

5. Serve immediately for best results.

Strawberry Smoothie

Serves: 4
Preparation time: 5 minutes
Calories/serving: 126

Ingredients

350 g / 12 oz / 2 ⅓ cups strawberries, hulled
2 ripe bananas, chopped
250 g / 9 oz / 1 cup plain yoghurt
110 ml / 4 fl. oz / ½ cup semi-skimmed milk
250 g / 9 oz / 1 cup crushed ice

Method

1. Combine the strawberries, banana, yoghurt and milk in a blender.

2. Blitz until smooth, then add the crushed ice.

3. Blitz again before pouring into glasses. Serve immediately for best results.

Scrambled Eggs with Mushrooms

Serves: 4
Preparation time: 5 minutes
Cooking time: 10 minutes
Calories/serving: 177

Ingredients

2 tbsp unsalted butter

150 g / 5 oz / 2 cups button mushrooms, sliced

6 large eggs

75 ml / 3 fl. oz / ⅓ cup fat-free milk

a small bunch of flat-leaf parsley

salt and freshly ground black pepper

Method

1. Add 1 tbsp of butter to a large sauté pan set over a moderate heat until hot.

2. Add the mushrooms and seasoning. Sauté for 5–6 minutes, stirring and tossing occasionally, until tender and starting to brown.

3. Meanwhile, whisk together the eggs with the milk and the remaining butter, then pour into a heavy-based saucepan set over a medium heat.

4. Cook, stirring frequently, until the egg starts to scramble and thicken.

5. Once cooked, season to taste and finely chop some of the parsley. Stir the parsley through the eggs. Serve with the sautéed mushrooms on the side and the remaining parsley as a garnish.

Fresh Fruit Salad

Serves: 2
Preparation time: 10–15 minutes
Calories/serving: 418

Ingredients

4 large kiwi fruit, peeled and sliced

300 g / 10 ½ oz / 2 cups strawberries

200 g / 7 oz / 1 ½ cups raspberries

1 mango, pitted and diced

½ lemon, juiced

2 tbsp gluten-free rolled oats

2 tbsp fromage frais

a sprig of mint

Method

1. Toss the fruit with the lemon juice in a large mixing bowl.

2. Spread out on a platter, building the fruit towards the centre.

3. Sprinkle over the rolled oats and spoon over the fromage frais.

4. Garnish with a sprig of mint before serving.

Salmon Coddled Egg

Serves: 4
Preparation time: 5 minutes
Cooking time: 3–4 minutes
Calories/serving: 144

Ingredients

1 tbsp unsalted butter

100 g / 3 ½ oz / ⅔ cup smoked salmon trimmings

4 large eggs

salt and freshly ground black pepper

a few sprigs of tarragon, to garnish

Method

1. Grease four heatproof ramekins with the butter, then arrange the smoked salmon trimmings in each ramekin. Crack an egg into the ramekins.

2. Season well, then place the ramekins in a large, heavy-based saucepan or casserole dish.

3. Pour in enough boiling water around the ramekins to reach halfway up their sides.

4. Cover the saucepan with a lid and cook over a low heat for 3–4 minutes until the eggs are set.

5. Remove from the saucepan and serve immediately with a sprig of tarragon on top as a garnish.

Raspberry-verbena Smoothie

Serves: 4
Preparation time: 5 minutes
Cooking time: 5 minutes
Calories/serving: 153

Ingredients

2 tbsp runny honey

a small bunch lemon verbena

450 g / 1 lb / 4 cups raspberries

250 ml / 9 fl. oz / 1 cup semi-skimmed milk

150 g / 5 oz / ⅔ cup low-fat plain yoghurt

Method

1. Warm the honey in a saucepan with a few sprigs of lemon verbena.

2. Add the warmed honey to a blender along with the raspberries, milk and yoghurt.

3. Blitz until smooth before pouring into glasses.

4. Serve with a garnish of lemon verbena.

Overnight Oats

Serves: 4
Preparation time: 5–10 minutes
+ overnight chilling
Calories/serving: 190

Ingredients

110 g / 4 oz / 1 ¼ cups gluten-free rolled oats
125 ml / 4 ½ fl. oz / ½ cup cold water
125 ml / 4 ½ fl. oz / ½ cup semi-skimmed milk
1 tbsp sultanas
1 small Red Delicious apple, roughly grated
55 g / 2 oz / ¼ cup fat-free plain yoghurt
75 g / 3 oz / ½ cup raspberries
55 g / 2 oz / ⅓ cup blueberries
1 tbsp sunflower seeds

Method

1. Combine the oats, water, milk and sultanas in a bowl and stir well; cover and chill overnight.

2. The next morning, stir in the grated apple and spoon the oat mixture into serving bowls.

3. Top with a dollop of yoghurt, a few raspberries and blueberries and a sprinkling of sunflower seeds.

4. Serve immediately for best results.

Pineapple and Mango Smoothie

Serves: 4
Preparation time: 10–15 minutes
Calories/serving: 157

Ingredients

1 small pineapple, peeled and cored

1 ripe mango, pitted

a few drops of vanilla extract

250 g / 9 oz / 1 cup plain yoghurt

150 ml / 5 fl. oz / ⅔ cup unsweetened almond milk

250 g / 9 oz / 1 cup crushed ice

Method

1. Chop the pineapple and mango flesh, then add to a blender along with the vanilla extract, yoghurt and milk.

2. Blitz until smooth before adding the crushed ice and then blitz again.

3. Pour into glasses and serve immediately for best results.

Asparagus Soup

Serves: 4
Preparation time: 10–15 minutes
Cooking time: 35–40 minutes
Calories/serving: 209

Ingredients

2 tbsp sunflower oil

1 shallot, finely chopped

500 g / 1 lb 2 oz / 4 cups white asparagus spears, trimmed, peeled and chopped

750 ml / 1 pint 6 fl. oz / 3 cups vegetable stock

100 g / 3 ½ oz / ½ cup crème fraiche

1 tbsp sherry

salt and freshly ground black pepper

1 tbsp white wine vinegar

4 medium eggs

a small handful of pea shoots, to garnish

Method

1. Heat the oil in a large saucepan set over a medium heat until hot. Add the shallot and sweat for 3–4 minutes until softened.

2. Add the asparagus and continue to cook for 4–5 minutes, stirring occasionally.

3. Cover with the stock and bring to a simmer. Cook steadily for 20–25 minutes, then blend with a stick blender or in a food processor until smooth.

4. Return the soup to a simmer and stir through the crème fraiche and sherry, then season to taste. Add the vinegar to a saucepan of simmering water.

5. Poach the eggs for 3 minutes before removing; ladle the soup into bowls and serve with the eggs, pea shoots and some pepper.

Fruity Muesli Yoghurt

Serves: 4
Preparation time: 10 minutes
Cooking time: 4 minutes
Calories/serving: 451

Ingredients

75 g / 3 oz / ¾ cup hazelnuts (cobnuts)
150 g / 5 oz / 1 ½ cups gluten-free rolled oats
100 g / 3 ½ oz / ⅔ cup raisins
750 g / 1 lb 10 oz / 3 cups plain yoghurt
2 medium nectarines, pitted and sliced
2 tbsp runny honey

Method

1. Place a dry frying pan over a medium heat. Add the hazelnuts and toast briefly until they give off a nutty aroma.

2. Stir into the oats and raisins in a mixing bowl.

3. Fill serving bowls with the yoghurt before topping with slices of nectarine, a drizzle of honey and spoonfuls of the muesli, then serve.

Mini Waffles

Serves: 6–8
Preparation time: 10 minutes
Cooking time: 10–15 minutes
Calories/serving: 351–263

Ingredients

300 g / 10 ½ oz / 2 cups gluten-free plain (all-purpose) flour

1 tbsp gluten-free baking powder

½ tsp Xanthan gum

2 tbsp icing (confectioners') sugar, to dust

½ tsp salt

2 large eggs, beaten

375 ml / 13 fl. oz / 1 ½ cups semi-skimmed milk

75 g / 3 oz / ⅓ cup unsalted butter, melted

1 tbsp sunflower oil, for greasing

Method

1. Mix the flour, baking powder, Xanthan gum, icing sugar and salt in a large mixing bowl and then beat together the eggs, milk and melted butter in a measuring jug.

2. Slowly add to the dry ingredients, whisking at the same time until you have a smooth batter.

3. Preheat a mini waffle iron and wipe the surface with a little sunflower oil.

4. Ladle the batter into the iron and close; cook according to manufacturer's instructions until the waffles are golden and set.

5. Repeat this method to cook the remaining batter until you have used all the batter.

6. Serve hot from the iron for best results.

Cherry Chocolate Smoothies

Serves: 4
Preparation time: 5 minutes
Calories/serving: 124

Ingredients

150 g / 5 oz / 1 cup strawberries, hulled
and chopped

450 g / 1 lb / 3 cups red cherries, pitted

250 g / 9 oz / 1 cup crushed ice

2 tbsp dark chocolate

Method

1. Combine the strawberries and cherries in a blender. Blitz until smooth.

2. Add the crushed ice and blitz again before pouring into glasses.

3. Grate some dark chocolate curls, sprinkle over the top and serve immediately.

Italian Coddled Eggs

Serves: 4
Preparation time: 15 minutes
Cooking time: 5 minutes
Calories/serving: 213

Ingredients

2 tbsp olive oil

4 slices of prosciutto

75 g / 3 oz / ½ cup cherry tomatoes, halved

4 large eggs

2 tbsp Parmesan, finely grated

2 tbsp balsamic vinegar

a few sprigs of thyme

salt and freshly ground black pepper

Method

1. Grease four individual ramekins with olive oil, then line with the prosciutto and cherry tomatoes before cracking the eggs in.

2. Top with Parmesan, balsamic vinegar, thyme and seasoning, then place in a large saucepan.

3. Fill the saucepan with boiling water so that it reaches halfway up the sides of the ramekins. Place the saucepan over a medium heat and cover with a lid.

4. Leave the eggs to cook for 3–4 minutes until set.

5. Once set, carefully remove from the saucepan before serving with a garnish of thyme.

Light Bites and Lunches

These days most of us are used to just grabbing a sandwich, or whatever else is available, at lunchtime. If you're avoiding gluten, you may not always be able to find gluten-free options at a café or sandwich bar. Even if you can, they're not always the healthiest choice.

If you're serious about improving your health, it's worth taking the time and effort to have a nutritious lunch. It will set you up until your evening meal, and keep you from wanting to snack in the afternoon. Why not make a big batch of gluten-free soup and freeze individual portions? It's easy and inexpensive, and you can heat it up at the office for a quick, healthy lunch.

The lunch ideas in this section can be eaten at other times of the day, and would even work as dinners. Mix and match and see which ones work best for you!

Vegetarian Bruschetta

Serves: 4
Preparation time: 10 minutes
Cooking time: 5 minutes
Calories/serving: 271

Ingredients

1 large cucumber, deseeded and finely diced
2 tbsp olive oil
350 g / 12 oz / 1 ½ cups cottage cheese
4 thick slices of multigrain bread
½ small iceberg lettuce, chopped
150 g / 5 oz / 1 cup radishes, sliced
a small bunch of dill, roughly chopped
2 tbsp pine nuts
a small handful of frisée lettuce
salt and freshly ground black pepper

Method

1. Dress the cucumber with the olive oil. Add the cottage cheese and stir well to combine, then season to taste.

2. Preheat the grill to hot; toast the slices of bread for a minute on both sides or until lightly browned before removing.

3. Top the toasted bread with some iceberg lettuce, then spoon over the cottage cheese mixture. Garnish with sliced radish, chopped dill, pine nuts and frisée before serving.

Smoked Fish Wraps

Serves: 4
Preparation time: 20 minutes
Calories/serving: 244

Ingredients

300 g / 10 ½ oz / 2 cups skinless halibut fillet, sliced thinly

½ lemon, juiced

salt and freshly ground black pepper

2 large gluten-free tortilla wraps

250 g / 9 oz / 1 ⅔ cups smoked salmon slices

1 head of Romaine lettuce, leaves separated

a large bunch of chives

3 tbsp salmon roe

Method

1. Dress the halibut slices with lemon juice, salt and pepper; leave to sit for 10 minutes.

2. Lay the tortillas on a flat surface, then layer slices of salmon and dressed halibut on top.

3. Top with lettuce leaves before laying the chives in bunches down the centre.

4. Roll up the wraps and cut into pieces. Arrange on a serving platter and serve with the salmon roe spooned over.

Dressed Asparagus Salad

Serves: 4
Preparation time: 10 minutes
Cooking time: 5 minutes
Calories/serving: 186

Ingredients

75 g / 3 oz / ⅓ cup plain yoghurt

2 tbsp mayonnaise

1 tbsp hot water

½ tsp paprika

salt and freshly ground black pepper

450 g / 1 lb / 4 cups asparagus spears, woody ends removed

150 g / 5 oz / 1 cup roast pork slices

2 tbsp baby capers in brine, drained

a large handful of rocket (arugula)

Method

1. Whisk together the yoghurt, mayonnaise, hot water and paprika in a small bowl; season and set to one side.

2. Cook the asparagus in a large saucepan of salted, boiling water for 3–4 minutes until tender, then refresh immediately in iced water.

3. Once cool, drain and pat dry, and then arrange on plates.

4. Top with folded slices of pork, baby capers and rocket leaves, then dress with the yoghurt sauce and a little more seasoning before serving.

Salmon Mousse Wraps

Serves: 4
Preparation time: 10–15 minutes
Cooking time: 15 minutes
Calories/serving: 455

Ingredients

450 g / 1 lb / 3 cups skinless salmon fillet

110 ml / 4 fl. oz / ½ cup dry white wine

1 bay leaf

1 tsp black peppercorns

100 ml / 3 ½ fl. oz / ½ cup double (heavy) cream

1 tsp Dijon mustard

1 large avocado, pitted and diced

½ lemon, juiced

4 gluten-free tortilla wraps

a large bunch of salad cress, snipped

salt and freshly ground black pepper

Method

1. Place the salmon in a large saucepan and add the wine, bay leaf, peppercorns and enough water to just cover.

2. Bring to a simmer over a moderate heat, then cover and reduce the heat to low. Cook for 6–8 minutes until cooked through.

3. Remove the salmon from the saucepan and flake into a food processor. Add half the cream and blitz until smooth, then add the mustard and more cream and blend as necessary. Season before leaving to cool.

4. Mash the avocado with lemon juice and seasoning until smooth, then spread over the wraps and top with the salmon mousse and cress.

5. Roll into wraps and serve immediately for best results.

Mixed Bean Soup

Serves: 4
Preparation time: 15 minutes
Cooking time: 30–35 minutes
Calories/serving: 463

Ingredients

2 tbsp olive oil

1 large onion, chopped

salt and freshly ground black pepper

600 g / 1 lb 5 oz / 4 cup floury potatoes,
peeled and roughly chopped

200 g / 7 oz / 1 cup canned chickpeas
(garbanzo beans), drained

400 g / 14 oz / 2 cups canned borlotti
beans, drained

100 g / 3 ½ oz / ½ cup adzuki beans, soaked
in water overnight

1.25 l / 2 pints 4 fl. oz / 5 cups vegetable stock

1 small head of broccoli, prepared into
small florets

2–3 tbsp balsamic vinegar

Method

1. Heat the olive oil in a large saucepan set
   over a medium heat until hot. Add the
   onion and a little salt, sweating for 4–5
   minutes until softened.

2. Add the potatoes and beans, then stir well
   and cook for 3 minutes.

3. Cover with the stock and bring to a
   simmer; cook steadily for 15 minutes,
   then add the broccoli.

4. Simmer the soup for a further 8–10 minutes
   until the beans and broccoli are tender.

5. Season to taste with balsamic vinegar,
   salt and freshly ground pepper before
   serving.

Warm Buckwheat Salad

Serves: 4
Preparation time: 10 minutes
Cooking time: 30–35 minutes
Calories/serving: 194

Ingredients

2 tbsp sunflower oil

1 tbsp unsalted butter

150 g / 5 oz / 2 cups closed cup
mushrooms, sliced

175 g / 6 oz / 1 cup buckwheat

500 ml / 18 fl. oz / 2 cups vegetable stock

a few sprigs of chervil, to garnish

salt and freshly ground black pepper

Method

1. Heat together the oil and butter in a large
   casserole dish set over a moderate heat.
   Add the mushrooms and a little salt and
   sauté for 5–6 minutes until lightly browned.

2. Add the buckwheat, stir well, and cover
   with the stock before bringing to the boil.

3. Reduce to a simmer for 20–25 minutes until
   most of the stock has been absorbed and
   the buckwheat is tender.

4. Season to taste with salt and pepper before
   serving in bowls with a garnish of chervil.

Cod and Lentils

Serves: 4
Preparation time: 10 minutes
Cooking time: 20–25 minutes
Calories/serving: 414

Ingredients

150 g / 5 oz / ¾ cup orange lentils

750 ml / 1 pint 6 fl. oz / 3 cups vegetable stock

4 x 175 g / 6 oz skinless cod fillets

3 tbsp olive oil

flaked sea salt and freshly ground black pepper

a few sprigs of basil, to garnish

5–6 cloves of garlic

1 large shallot, finely sliced

a few sprigs of coriander (cilantro), to garnish

Method

1. Combine the lentils and stock in a saucepan. Bring to boiling point and cook steadily for 5 minutes, then reduce to a simmer for 15–20 minutes until tender.

2. Preheat the oven to 220°C (200°C fan) / 425F / gas 7 and line a baking tray with greaseproof paper.

3. Rub the cod with olive oil and season generously; place on the tray. Finely slice a few basil leaves and scatter over the cod, tucking the garlic around the fish.

4. Roast for 10–12 minutes until the flesh is firm yet slightly springy to the touch.

5. Leave to rest briefly before serving over a bed of lentils, garnished with shallot, coriander and the remaining basil.

Mixed Lettuce Salad

Serves: 4
Preparation time: 10–15 minutes
Calories/serving: 283

Ingredients

3 tbsp buttermilk

1 tbsp mayonnaise

1 tsp black poppy seeds

salt and freshly ground black pepper

150 g / 5 oz / 3 cups curly kale

½ white cabbage, sliced

1 head of radicchio, chopped

2 oranges, peeled and sliced

2 white grapefruit, sliced

75 g / 3 oz / ¾ cup pumpkin seeds

75 g / 3 oz / ½ cup dried cranberries

Method

1. Whisk together the buttermilk, mayonnaise and poppy seeds with a little seasoning.

2. Toss together the kale, cabbage and radicchio, then arrange in serving bowls.

3. Serve with the citrus fruit, pumpkin seeds, cranberries, and buttermilk dressing on the side.

Asian Leek Soup

Serves: 4
Preparation time: 10 minutes
Cooking time: 20 minutes
Calories/serving: 127

Ingredients

2 tbsp groundnut oil

1 large leek, finely sliced

1 l / 1 pint 16 fl. oz / 4 cups fish stock

450 g / 1 lb / 3 cups prawns (shrimp), peeled
with tails intact

1 large egg white, lightly beaten

1 tbsp rice wine vinegar

1 tbsp fish sauce

salt and freshly ground black pepper

1 lime, sliced

a small handful of salad cress, to garnish

Method

1. Heat the oil in a large saucepan set over a
   medium heat. Add the leek and a little salt,
   sweating for 5–6 minutes until softened.

2. Cover with the fish stock and bring to a
   simmer; cook steadily for 5 minutes, then
   add the prawns.

3. Continue to cook for 5 minutes until they
   are pink and tender, then stir through the
   egg white and simmer for 2 minutes.

4. Season to taste with rice wine vinegar,
   fish sauce, salt and pepper before ladling
   into soup bowls.

5. Garnish with slices of lime and cress
   before serving.

Gluten-free Fougasse

Serves: 8
Preparation time:
  25 minutes plus proving
Cooking time: 18–22 minutes
Calories/serving: 337

Ingredients

350 ml / 12 fl. oz / 1 ½ cups warm water

1 ½ tsp gluten-free dried yeast

450 g / 1 lb / 3 cups gluten-free plain (all-purpose) flour, plus extra for dusting

¾ tsp Xanthan gum

110 ml / 4 fl. oz / ½ cup olive oil

75 g / 3 oz / ½ cup pitted black olives

1 tbsp coriander (cilantro) seeds

a few sprigs of rosemary, to garnish

salt and freshly ground black pepper

Method

1. Pour the water into a bowl and sprinkle in the yeast. Leave to dissolve before adding 110 g / 4 oz / ⅔ cup of the flour along with the Xanthan gum and oil.

2. Stir well, then add the remaining flour in thirds, until the dough is tacky; knead on a floured surface until elastic.

3. Shape into a ball, place in a bowl and leave to prove in a warm place, covered loosely, for 60 minutes.

4. Knock back the dough then shape into four flat rounds, and stud with olives and coriander seeds.

5. Preheat the oven to 190°C (170°C fan) / 375F / gas 5; bake on a lined tray for 18–22 minutes until golden.

6. Garnish with rosemary before serving.

Lentil Pea Salad

Serves: 4
Preparation time: 10 minutes
Cooking time: 30–35 minutes
Calories/serving: 406

Ingredients

300 g / 10 ½ oz / 1 ⅓ cups green lentils
1.25 l / 2 pints 4 fl. oz / 5 cups
  vegetable stock
225 g / 8 oz / 2 cups frozen peas
225 g / 8 oz / 2 cups runner beans, chopped
2 tbsp sherry vinegar
2 tbsp extra-virgin olive oil
2 plum tomatoes, deseeded and diced
1 orange
salt and freshly ground black pepper

Method

1. Cover the lentils with the stock in a large saucepan; bring to boiling point and cook rapidly for 5 minutes, then simmer for 18–22 minutes until tender.

2. Once tender, drain well and leave to cool to one side.

3. Blanch the peas and runner beans in a large saucepan of salted, boiling water for 2–3 minutes until tender. Drain and add to the lentils in a large mixing bowl.

4. Add the sherry vinegar, oil and tomatoes; toss well before seasoning to taste.

5. Spoon into bowls and sprinkle with some freshly grated orange zest before serving.

Green Tea Tofu

Serves: 4
Preparation time:
  10 minutes plus chilling
Cooking time: 10 minutes
Calories/serving: 171

Ingredients

250 ml / 9 fl. oz / 1 cup hot water

2 green tea bags

a pinch of caster (superfine) sugar

75 ml / 3 fl. oz / ⅓ cup double (heavy) cream

450 g / 1 lb / 3 cups firm tofu, cut into
  large cubes

a small bunch of alfalfa sprouts, to garnish

2 tsp white sesame seeds

1 tbsp pine nuts, sliced

salt and freshly ground black pepper

Method

1. Place the water in a small saucepan.
   Add the green tea and bring to a simmer,
   then remove from the heat and leave to
   brew for 5 minutes.

2. Strain the tea back into the saucepan and
   bring to boiling point; add the sugar and
   cream, then simmer.

3. Season to taste and leave to cool, then chill
   until cold.

4. Serve the cold sauce over cubes of tofu
   and a garnish of alfalfa sprouts, sesame
   seeds and pine nuts.

Cheesy Aubergine Cakes

Makes: 8
Preparation time: 15 minutes
Cooking time: 55–60 minutes
Calories/serving: 353

Ingredients

750 g / 1 lb 10 oz / 5 cups floury potatoes, peeled and diced

2 tbsp cornflour (cornstarch)

salt and freshly ground black pepper

2 tbsp sunflower oil

1 large aubergine (eggplant), finely diced

100 g / 3 ½ oz / ⅔ cup sun-dried tomato, drained and chopped

225 g / 8 oz / 2 cups mozzarella, cut into 8 slices

225 g / 8 oz / 2 cups golden breadcrumbs

2 tbsp black poppy seeds

2 tbsp olive oil

a small bunch of rocket (arugula) leaves, to garnish

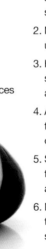

Method

1. Cook the potato in a large saucepan of salted, boiling water for 18–22 minutes until soft; drain well and leave to cool briefly.

2. Mash with the cornflour and seasoning until smooth.

3. Heat the sunflower oil in a large frying pan set over a moderate heat, then sauté the aubergine with a little salt for 5–6 minutes.

4. Add to the potato along with the sun-dried tomato before mashing again. Preheat the oven to 200°C (180°C fan) / 400F / gas 6.

5. Shape into 8 cakes around the mozzarella, then coat in a mixture of the breadcrumbs and poppy seeds.

6. Drizzle with olive oil, then bake on lined trays for 20–25 minutes until golden before serving with rocket.

Spinach and Potato Soup

Serves: 4
Preparation time: 15 minutes
Cooking time: 30–35 minutes
Calories/serving: 245

Ingredients

2 tbsp unsalted butter

1 tbsp olive oil

1 large onion, finely chopped

750 g / 1 lb 10 oz / 5 cups floury potatoes, peeled and sliced

1 l / 1 pint 16 fl. oz / 4 cups vegetable stock

110 ml / 4 fl. oz / ½ cup whole milk

150 g / 5 oz / 3 cups baby spinach, washed

salt and freshly ground black pepper

½ tsp paprika, to garnish

Method

1. Heat the butter and oil in a large saucepan set over a medium heat until hot. Add the onion and a little salt, sweating for 5–6 minutes before adding the potato.

2. Cook for 4–5 minutes, then cover with the stock and milk.

3. Bring to a simmer and cook for 15 minutes until the potato is soft. Stir through half the spinach and cook for 1 minute.

4. Remove some of the potato from the soup, then blend with a stick blender or in a food processor until smooth.

5. Return the soup to a simmer before adding the rest of the spinach and the reserved potato.

6. Season to taste before serving with a garnish of paprika.

Main Meals

You've stuck to your gluten-free diet for breakfast and lunch and now it's time for a delicious dinner – you deserve it!

The core of any nutritious dinner is a mix of protein, vegetables and starchy grains. You can easily achieve this with gluten-free foods, and if you can also make it low-fat and low-sugar, that's even better! Fish, lean meats and pulses are the best way to meet your protein needs and they're easy to cook in a variety of different ways.

Vegetables are a no-brainer on any diet. They're gluten-free, low in fat and sugar, and packed with nutrients. The starches on your dinner plate can be provided by a range of gluten-free foods: potatoes, rice, sweet potatoes and quinoa are just a few of the options. If you're missing pasta, treat yourself to the gluten-free version occasionally. The recipes in this section will give you a lot of great ideas, so why not start to experiment with something new?

Monkfish Kebabs

Serves: 4
Preparation time: 10 minutes
Cooking time: 10 minutes
Calories/serving: 257

Ingredients

1 tsp ground cumin

1 tsp paprika

salt and freshly ground black pepper

2 tbsp sesame seeds

600 g / 1 lb 5 oz / 4 cups monkfish tail, diced evenly

55 ml / 2 fl. oz / ¼ cup olive oil

a few sprigs of flat-leaf parsley, to garnish

lime wedges, to garnish

wooden skewers, soaked in cold water for 30 minutes beforehand

Method

1. Preheat the grill to a moderately hot temperature. Combine the ground spices with seasoning and sesame seeds in a shallow dish.

2. Toss the monkfish pieces in the olive oil until evenly covered.

3. Roll in the sesame seed mixture, and then thread carefully onto the wooden skewers.

4. Arrange on a grill tray; cook for 5–6 minutes, turning frequently, until the fish is firm yet slightly springy to the touch.

5. Remove and arrange on serving plates. Garnish with the sprigs of parsley and lime wedges before serving.

Spiced Courgette Gratin

Serves: 4
Preparation time: 10 minutes
Cooking time: 10 minutes
Calories/serving: 333

Ingredients

4 large courgettes (zucchinis), thinly sliced
225 g / 8 oz / 1 cup light mayonnaise
225 g / 8 oz / 1 cup plain yoghurt
salt and freshly ground black pepper
1 tbsp cumin seeds
a pinch of fennel seeds
75 g / 3 oz / ¾ cup Parmesan, grated
2 tbsp olive oil

Method

1. Cook the courgette in a large saucepan of salted, boiling water for 2 minutes; drain and leave to cool.

2. Preheat the grill to a moderately hot temperature.

3. Whisk together the mayonnaise and yoghurt with salt and pepper, then spoon into the base of a gratin or baking dish.

4. Layer slices of courgette over the sauce and sprinkle over the cumin seeds, fennel seeds and Parmesan. Drizzle with olive oil.

5. Grill for 3–4 minutes until golden and bubbling; remove from the grill before serving.

Baked Thai Chicken

Serves: 4
Preparation time: 15 minutes
Cooking time: 30–35 minutes
Calories/serving: 205

Ingredients

55 ml / 2 fl. oz / ¼ cup sunflower oil

3 tbsp rice wine vinegar

2 tbsp fish sauce

1 tbsp caster (superfine) sugar

4 large skinless chicken breasts, halved

4 lemongrass stalks, lightly crushed

8 stalks of celery, trimmed and halved

4 red chillies (chilies), sliced

a few sprigs of coriander (cilantro), to garnish

Method

1. Preheat the oven to 190°C (170°C fan) / 375F / gas 5. Whisk together the oil, vinegar, fish sauce and sugar in a small mixing bowl until the sugar dissolves.

2. Cut 4 square sheets of greaseproof paper. Arrange the chicken pieces, lemongrass, celery and chilli in the centre of each sheet.

3. Bring the edges up and around the ingredients, then pour over the prepared sauce.

4. Seal the edges of the paper together by crimping. Sit the parcels on a large baking tray.

5. Bake for 22–25 minutes until the chicken is cooked through. Carefully open the parcels before serving with a garnish of coriander.

Poached Cod Fillet

Serves: 4
Preparation time: 15 minutes
Cooking time: 20 minutes
Calories/serving: 367

Ingredients

2 tbsp unsalted butter

1 leek, roughly sliced

1 fennel bulb, sliced

2 large carrots, peeled and sliced

salt

250 ml / 9 fl. oz / 1 cup fish stock

110 ml / 4 fl. oz / ½ cup double (heavy) cream

4 x 175 g / 6 oz cod fillets

1 tbsp fennel seeds

a small handful of watercress, to garnish

1 tsp orange zest, to garnish

Method

1. Heat the butter in a large casserole dish set over a medium heat until hot. Add the leek, fennel and carrot, sweating with a little salt for 8–10 minutes until soft.

2. Remove from the dish and keep warm to one side.

3. Add the stock to the dish and bring to a simmer, then add the cream; return the broth to a simmer.

4. Position the cod fillets in the broth and cover with a lid; cook for 6–8 minutes until the fish is firm yet slightly springy to the touch.

5. Spoon into serving bowls and garnish with the sweated vegetables, fennel seeds, watercress and a pinch of orange zest.

Summer Veal Kebabs

Serves: 4
Preparation time: 15 minutes
Cooking time: 10 minutes
Calories/serving: 285

Ingredients

1 small head of hispi cabbage, diced

1 yellow pepper, deseeded and diced

450 g / 1 lb / 3 cups veal fillet, diced

75 g / 3 oz / 1 cup button mushrooms, halved

4 wooden skewers, soaked in water for 30 minutes beforehand

55 ml / 2 fl. oz / ¼ cup sunflower oil

1 tbsp cumin seeds

salt and freshly ground black pepper

1 plum tomato, deseeded and finely diced

Method

1. Preheat the grill to a moderately hot temperature, then thread the cabbage, pepper, veal and mushrooms onto the skewers, alternating as necessary.

2. Brush with the oil before sprinkling over the cumin seeds. Season with plenty of salt and pepper.

3. Arrange on a grilling tray and cook under the grill for 6–8 minutes, turning occasionally, until the veal is cooked through and the vegetables are lightly browned.

4. Allow the kebabs to rest for a few minutes before serving with a tomato garnish on top.

Spiced Chicken Kebabs

Serves: 4
Preparation time: 25 minutes
Cooking time: 15 minutes
Calories/serving: 91

Ingredients

2 courgettes (zucchinis)

2 large skinless chicken breasts, trimmed

2 tbsp sunflower oil

2 tbsp gluten-free light soy sauce

2 tsp red peppercorns, lightly crushed

1 lemon, cut into wedges

8 small wooden skewers, soaked in cold
water for 30 minutes beforehand

Method

1. Peel strips from the courgettes to leave a striped pattern, then slice into thick coins, and cook in a saucepan of salted, boiling water for 3–4 minutes until tender. Drain well.

2. Preheat the grill to a moderately hot temperature. Cut each chicken breast into 4 fingers and place in a large mixing bowl.

3. Add the sunflower oil, soy sauce and peppercorns; mix well to coat and leave for 10 minutes.

4. Thread the pieces of chicken onto wooden skewers and grill on a tray for 7–8 minutes, turning once, until the chicken is firm and cooked through.

5. Serve the kebabs with the courgette and lemon wedges on the side.

Mediterranean Tuna Kebabs

Serves: 4
Preparation time: 10–15 minutes
Cooking time: 10 minutes
Calories/serving: 398

Ingredients

600 g / 1 lb 5 oz / 4 cups tuna fillet, cubed

4 wooden skewers, soaked in water for
   30 minutes beforehand

4 slices of prosciutto, folded

2 small vine tomatoes, cored and halved

1 large onion, chopped

55 ml / 2 fl. oz / ¼ cup olive oil

salt and freshly ground black pepper

a small bunch of basil leaves, sliced

1 lemon, sliced

Method

1. Preheat the grill to hot and then thread the
   tuna onto the skewers, alternating with
   the folded slices of prosciutto, tomato and
   onion.

2. Brush liberally with olive oil and season
   with salt and pepper, then sprinkle with
   some of the basil and arrange on a grilling
   tray.

3. Cook under the grill for 6–8 minutes,
   turning occasionally, until the tuna is lightly
   browned all over.

4. Remove from the grill and serve with more
   basil and lemon slices as a garnish.

Creamy Seafood Pasta

Serves: 4
Preparation time: 10–15 minutes
Cooking time: 20 minutes
Calories/serving: 553

Ingredients

2 tbsp olive oil

1 onion, finely chopped

300 g / 10 ½ oz / 2 cups prawns (shrimp), peeled

110 ml / 4 fl. oz / ½ cup double (heavy) cream

2 tbsp dried prawns (shrimp), chopped

55 g / 2 oz / 1 cup dried chopped seaweed,
  soaked in hot water and drained

½ lemon, juiced

salt and freshly ground black pepper

350 g / 12 oz / 3 cups gluten-free tagliatelle

mixed herbs, to garnish

Method

1. Heat the oil in a sauté pan set over a medium heat until hot; add the onion and sweat for 4–5 minutes.

2. Add the prawns and cook for 3–4 minutes until tender. Add to the food processor with the cream.

3. Pulse until finely chopped, then return to the sauté pan and add the dried prawns, seaweed, lemon juice and seasoning. Set to one side.

4. Cook the tagliatelle in a large saucepan of salted, boiling water until 'al dente', for 8–10 minutes.

5. Drain and reserve some of the cooking liquid. Add to the sauté pan and toss well over a medium heat.

6. Serve in bowls garnished with mixed herbs.

Veal Marengo Stew

Serves: 4
Preparation time: 10 minutes
Cooking time: 45–50 minutes
Calories/serving: 304

Ingredients

2 tbsp olive oil

450 g / 1 lb / 3 cups veal fillet, diced

salt and freshly ground black pepper

1 onion, finely chopped

1 clove of garlic, minced

110 g / 4 oz / 1 ½ cups white
mushrooms, sliced

½ tsp dried basil

½ tsp dried oregano

400 g / 14 oz / 2 cups canned
chopped tomatoes

400 ml / 14 fl. oz / 1 ⅔ cups light beef stock

Method

1. Heat the olive oil in a large casserole dish
   set over a moderate heat until hot. Season
   the veal and seal, in batches if necessary,
   until golden.

2. Remove from the dish, then add the onion,
   garlic and mushrooms.

3. Sauté for 3–4 minutes, then add the dried
   herbs and stir in the chopped tomatoes
   and beef stock.

4. Bring to a simmer before reducing the heat
   and cooking, uncovered, for 35–40 minutes
   until the veal is tender.

5. Adjust the seasoning to taste before ladling
   into bowls and serving.

Quick Biryani

Serves: 4
Preparation time: 20 minutes
Cooking time: 25–30 minutes
Calories/serving: 273

Ingredients

3 tbsp sunflower oil

2 small onions, finely chopped

4 cloves of garlic, minced

2 tbsp Madras curry powder

2 large plum tomatoes, deseeded and diced

225 g / 8 oz / 1 cup basmati rice, rinsed in several changes of water

450 ml / 16 fl. oz / 2 cups vegetable stock

salt and freshly ground black pepper

2 tbsp flaked (slivered) almonds, to garnish

a small bunch of coriander (cilantro), finely chopped

a few sprigs of thyme, to garnish

Method

1. Preheat the oven 180°C (160°C fan) / 350F / gas 4.

2. Heat the oil in a casserole dish set over a medium heat, then add the onion, garlic and a little salt.

3. Sweat for 8–10 minutes until golden, then add the curry powder and stir well.

4. Stir in the tomato and rice. Cover with the stock and simmer. Cover with a lid.

5. Transfer to the oven to finish cooking for 15–20 minutes until the rice has absorbed the stock and is plump.

6. Remove from the oven and leave to cool, covered, for 10 minutes before fluffing with a fork, stirring through the coriander and seasoning.

7. Serve garnished with almonds and thyme.

Hake with Beans

Serves: 4
Preparation time: 10 minutes
Cooking time: 10 minutes
Calories/serving: 214

Ingredients

4 x 150 g / 5 oz skinless hake fillet, pin-boned
2 tbsp unsalted butter, cubed
2 tsp coriander (cilantro) seeds
1 tsp dried thyme
225 g / 8 oz / 2 cups green (string) beans
125 g / 4 ½ oz / 1 cup mangetout
75 g / 3 oz / ¾ cup frozen peas
2 spring onions (scallions), sliced
a small bunch of flat-leaf parsley, chopped
salt and freshly ground black pepper

Method

1. Preheat the oven to 200°C (180°C fan) / 400F / gas 6, and then line a baking tray with greaseproof paper and place the hake on top.

2. Top with butter, coriander seeds, thyme, salt and pepper.

3. Roast for 8–10 minutes until firm yet slightly springy to the touch.

4. Cook the green beans, mangetout and peas in a large saucepan of salted, boiling water for 3 minutes. Drain and leave to cool.

5. Toss the beans with the spring onion, parsley and seasoning.

6. Serve on plates topped with the hake.

Asian Tofu Soup

Serves: 4
Preparation time: 10–15 minutes
Cooking time: 20 minutes
Calories/serving: 392

Ingredients

2 tbsp sunflower oil

1 small head of broccoli, prepared into small florets

1 large red pepper, deseeded and sliced

75 g / 3 oz / 1 cup mushrooms, sliced

1.25 l / 2 pint 4 fl. oz / 5 cups chicken stock

350 g / 12 oz / 2 ⅓ cups firm tofu, cubed

200 g / 7 oz / 1 cup canned sweetcorn, drained

250 g / 9 oz / 2 cups buckwheat vermicelli

2 tbsp dark soy sauce

2 tbsp rice wine vinegar

a small bunch of Thai basil, leaves picked

Method

1. Heat the oil in a large saucepan set over a moderate heat until hot; add the broccoli, red pepper and mushrooms.

2. Sauté for 2–3 minutes, then cover with stock. Bring to a simmer and add the tofu, sweetcorn and noodles.

3. Cook steadily for 12–14 minutes until the noodles are soft. Season to taste with soy sauce and rice vinegar before ladling into bowls.

4. Garnish with basil leaves before serving.

Roasted Grouper

Serves: 4
Preparation time: 10–15 minutes
Cooking time: 15 minutes
Calories/serving: 362

Ingredients

1 fennel bulb

3 tbsp unsalted butter, softened

salt and freshly ground black pepper

4 x 175 g / 6 oz grouper fillets

100 g / 3 ½ oz / ⅔ cup small scallops, roe removed

110 g / 4 oz / 1 cup asparagus spears, woody ends removed

150 g / 5 oz / 1 cup baby carrots, peeled

100 g / 3 ½ oz / 1 cup green (string) beans, trimmed

2 baby courgettes (zucchini), halved

2 tbsp olive oil

Method

1. Preheat the oven to 200°C (180°C fan) / 400F / gas 6 and line a baking tray with greaseproof paper.

2. Finely chop the fennel fronds and mix most of them with the butter and seasoning.

3. Place the grouper and scallops on the baking tray; top with the fennel butter and roast for 10–12 minutes until the fish is firm.

4. Meanwhile, cook the asparagus, carrots, courgette and green beans in a large saucepan of salted, boiling water for 3–4 minutes until tender. Drain and refresh in iced water.

5. Cut the asparagus in half and toss with the carrots, courgette, beans, olive oil and seasoning. Serve with the vegetables and scallops on the side.

Rabbit en Papillote

Serves: 4
Preparation time: 15 minutes
Cooking time: 45–50 minutes
Calories/serving: 566

Ingredients

4 large carrots, peeled and cut into batons
1 large white cabbage, shredded
4 small skinless rabbit legs, trimmed
55 ml / 2 fl. oz / ¼ cup olive oil
2 tbsp balsamic vinegar
a few sprigs of thyme

Method

1. Preheat the oven to 180°C (160°C fan) / 350F / gas 4 and cut 4 large rectangles of greaseproof paper.

2. Arrange the carrot and cabbage in the centre of the sheets of paper and sit the rabbit legs on top.

3. Drizzle over the olive oil and balsamic vinegar before topping with the thyme sprigs.

4. Bring the edges of the paper up and around the rabbit and seal well by crimping together.

5. Place on a baking tray and bake for 40–45 minutes until the rabbit is cooked through; remove from the oven and leave to cool slightly before opening and serving.

Baked Cod

Serves: 4
Preparation time: 15 minutes
Cooking time: 20 minutes
Calories/serving: 282

Ingredients

1 orange
100 g / 3 ½ oz / 2 cups baby spinach
4 x 175 g / 6 oz skinless cod fillets
2 tbsp olive oil
salt and freshly ground black pepper
200 g / 7 oz / 1 cup fromage frais

Method

1. Preheat the oven to 180°C (160°C fan) / 350F / gas 4 and then pare the zest from the orange and julienne.

2. Cut 4 rectangles of greaseproof paper and scatter the spinach leaves down the middle of each piece.

3. Sit the cod on top and drizzle with olive oil and seasoning. Bring the edges up and around the fish and seal well by folding together.

4. Place on a baking tray and bake for 18–20 minutes; the fish should feel firm with a little spring when poked through the paper.

5. Remove from the oven and open carefully before topping with fromage frais, orange zest and a little more pepper.

Roasted Autumn Vegetables

Serves: 4
Preparation time: 15 minutes
Cooking time: 45–55 minutes
Calories/serving: 355

Ingredients

1 small pumpkin, deseeded and cut into slices
4 large parsnips, peeled and quartered
2 red onions, chopped
1 butternut squash, deseeded and sliced
6 cloves of garlic, lightly crushed
a small bunch of thyme, chopped
75 ml / 3 fl. oz / ⅓ cup olive oil
salt and freshly ground black pepper

Method

1. Preheat the oven to 180°C (160°C fan) / 350F / gas 4.
2. Toss the vegetables and garlic with most of the thyme, then add the olive oil and seasoning and toss again.
3. Spread out across a large baking tray; roast for 45–55 minutes until tender and lightly browned.
4. Remove from the oven and garnish with the remaining thyme before serving.

Desserts

On the face of it, preparing a gluten-free dessert may seem like a tall order. If you're used to cakes, crumbles and pies, it may be hard to think of a dessert that doesn't use wheat flour.

You can substitute wheat flour for gluten-free flour in your recipes, but some will work better than others. Some sweet treats, such as brownies, actually work even better without flour, as they become richer and stickier.

There are a range of new ingredients to try. Rice, tapioca and potato flours all add texture to baking. Experiment until you find a recipe that you like! You can make delicious gluten-free cheesecakes and custard tarts by swapping out the wheat in the crust or base.

Some desserts, such as pavlova, use ingredients that are naturally gluten-free. Fresh seasonal fruit always makes a great dessert, or why not go for a selection of cheeses and gluten-free crackers?

White Chocolate Mousse

Makes: 8
Preparation time:
 20 minutes plus chilling
Cooking time: 15 minutes
Calories/serving: 302

Ingredients

250 g / 9 oz / 2 cups raspberries

65 g / 2 ½ oz / ½ cup icing (confectioners')
 sugar, sifted

1 lime, juiced

2 medium egg yolks

2 tbsp caster (superfine) sugar

300 ml / 10 ½ fl. oz / 1 ¼ cups double
 (heavy) cream

200 g / 7 oz / 1 ⅓ cups white chocolate,
 chopped

a few sprigs of mint, to garnish

Method

1. Cook the raspberries, icing sugar and lime
 juice in a saucepan over a medium heat
 until softened, then mash and leave to cool.

2. Beat together the egg yolks and sugar
 until thick. Heat 75 ml / 3 fl. oz / ⅓ cup of
 the cream in a saucepan until boiling, then
 pour over the egg mixture, whisking well.

3. Pour into a saucepan and cook over a low
 heat until it reaches a coating consistency.

4. Pour over the chocolate in a heatproof
 bowl and leave for 1 minute before stirring
 until smooth.

5. Whip the remaining cream until stiffly
 peaked, then fold into the melted chocolate
 in two batches before spooning into small
 glasses and chilling for 1 hour.

6. Top with raspberry coulis and mint leaves.

Chestnut Brûlées

Makes: 4
Preparation time: 5–10 minutes
Cooking time: 55–60 minutes
Calories/serving: 410

Ingredients

250 ml / 9 fl. oz / 1 cup whole milk

250 ml / 9 fl. oz / 1 cup double (heavy) cream

1 tsp vanilla extract

6 large egg yolks

55 g / 2 oz / ¼ cup caster (superfine) sugar

100 g / 3 ½ oz / ½ cup sweetened
  chestnut purée

Method

1. Preheat the oven to 150°C (130°C fan) /
   300F / gas 2. Combine the milk, cream and
   vanilla extract in a saucepan, bringing to a
   simmer over a moderate heat.

2. Whisk together the egg yolks, sugar and
   chestnut purée in a bowl until pale and
   thick.

3. Pour over the milk and cream in a slow,
   steady stream, whisking continuously
   until smooth.

4. Strain the mixture into a jug and pour into
   4 individual ramekins; sit them in a roasting
   tray and fill the tray with boiling water so
   that it comes halfway up their side.

5. Transfer to the oven for 45–50 minutes until
   set at the edges but with a slight wobble at
   the centre.

Strawberry Panna Cotta

Serves: 4
Preparation time:
 20 minutes plus chilling
Cooking time: 10 minutes
Calories/serving: 380

Ingredients

250 ml / 9 fl. oz / 1 cup double (heavy) cream

250 ml / 9 fl. oz / 1 cup whole milk

1 vanilla pod, split in half with seeds
 scraped out

2 tbsp caster (superfine) sugar

3 sheets of gelatine, soaked in cold water

300 g / 10 ½ oz / 2 cups strawberries, chopped

65 g / 2 ½ oz / ½ cup icing (confectioners')
 sugar

½ lemon, juiced

Method

1. Combine the cream, milk, vanilla pod (and
   seeds) and caster sugar in a saucepan;
   bring to a simmer over a medium heat
   before removing from the heat.

2. Squeeze the gelatine leaves dry and then
   add to the hot cream and milk and whisk
   until dissolved.

3. Leave to cool to room temperature, then
   divide between 4 glasses; cover and chill
   for at least 1 hour until set.

4. Meanwhile, combine most of the
   strawberries with the icing sugar and lemon
   juice in a saucepan; cook over a low heat
   until the fruit starts to soften.

5. Lightly mash with a fork before leaving to
   cool; serve over the panna cottas with the
   remaining strawberries on top.

Frozen Chocolate Lollies

Makes: 8
Preparation time: 10–15 minutes
Freezing time: 3 ½–4 ½ hours
Calories/serving: 277

Ingredients

4 large bananas, peeled and chopped

225 g / 8 oz / 1 cup plain yoghurt

150 g / 5 oz / 1 cup milk chocolate, chopped

100 g / 3 ½ oz / ⅔ cup dark chocolate, chopped

2 tsp liquid glucose

3 tbsp hazelnuts (cobnuts), chopped

Method

1. Blend the banana and yoghurt in a food processor until smooth. Scrape into a bowl.

2. Melt the chocolates and glucose in a heatproof bowl set over a saucepan of barely simmering water.

3. Stir occasionally until smooth, and then allow it to cool a little before whisking into the yoghurt mixture.

4. Pour evenly into an 8-hole ice-lolly mould and freeze for 1 hour until semi-frozen.

5. After 1 hour, insert ice-lolly sticks into the semi-frozen lollies. Return to the freezer for 2–3 hours until fully frozen.

6. Dip the bottom half of the mould into a bowl of hot water to loosen them. Serve with a sprinkle of chopped hazelnuts.

Yoghurt Eton Mess

Serves: 4
Preparation time: 10–15 minutes
Cooking time: 15 minutes
Calories/serving: 432

Ingredients

450 g / 1 lb / 3 cups strawberries,
hulled and chopped

100 g / 3 ½ oz / ¾ cup icing
(confectioners') sugar

1 lemon, juiced

750 g / 1 lb 10 oz / 3 cups Greek yoghurt

2 ready-made meringue nests, crushed

a few sprigs of mint, to garnish

Method

1. Combine the strawberries, icing sugar
   and lemon juice in a saucepan. Cook
   over a low heat, stirring occasionally, until
   softened and juicy.

2. Roughly mash with a fork, then spoon most
   of the strawberries into a food processor.
   Blitz until smooth.

3. Strain the purée through a fine sieve into
   a bowl. Add the yoghurt and whisk until
   thoroughly combined.

4. Divide the yoghurt between 4 glasses,
   then top with the remaining strawberries,
   crushed meringue and a garnish of mint
   before serving.

Chestnut Pancakes

Serves: 4
Preparation time: 10 minutes
Cooking time: 20–25 minutes
Calories/serving: 470

Ingredients

110 g / 4 oz / ⅔ cup chestnut flour
2 tbsp gluten-free plain (all-purpose) flour
a pinch of salt
1 tbsp caster (superfine) sugar
2 medium eggs, beaten
250 ml / 9 fl. oz / 1 cup semi-skimmed milk
55 g / 2 oz / ¼ cup butter, melted
150 g / 5 oz / 1 cup goats' cheese, cubed
400 g / 14 oz / 2 cups canned cherries
   in syrup

Method

1. Sift together the flours, salt and sugar into a large mixing bowl; whisk in the eggs, then add the milk gradually until smooth.

2. Whisk in 1 tbsp of melted butter. The rest will be used to grease the pan between cooking each crêpe.

3. Heat a crêpe pan over a medium heat and grease; add a small ladle of batter and tilt the pan to let it run all over.

4. Cook for 1 minute until set, then flip and cook for a further 30 seconds before sliding onto a plate. Repeat this method for the remaining crêpes, stacking once cooked.

5. Top the stacked crêpes with goats' cheese and cherries in their syrup before serving.

Speculoos Pear Tart

Serves: 8
Preparation time: 15 minutes
Cooking time: 25–30 minutes
Calories/serving: 368

Ingredients

250 g / 9 oz / 1 cup ready-made gluten-free shortcrust pastry

a little gluten-free plain (all-purpose) flour, for dusting

150 g / 5 oz / 1 cup speculoos biscuits

75 g / 3 oz / ⅓ cup unsalted butter, melted

3 tbsp caster (superfine) sugar

4 medium pears, peeled, cored and sliced

Method

1. Preheat the oven to 180°C (160°C fan) / 350F / gas 4. Roll out the pastry on a lightly floured surface to 1 cm (½ in) thickness and use to line and 20 cm (8 in) springform fluted tart tin.

2. Press well into the base and sides and trim the excess. Prick the base with a fork.

3. Pulse together the biscuits, melted butter and sugar in a food processor until they come together roughly.

4. Spread over the base of the pastry, then top with the slices of pear, overlapping them to fit as necessary.

5. Bake for 25–30 minutes until the pastry is cooked and golden at the edges before serving.

Roasted Vanilla Apricots

Serves: 4
Preparation time: 10–15 minutes
Cooking time: 35 minutes
Calories/serving: 136

Ingredients

800 g / 1 lb 12 oz / 4 cups canned apricots in syrup

2 vanilla pods, split

a few sprigs of lavender, chopped

2 limes, cut into wedges

a pinch of salt

Method

1. Preheat the oven to 190°C (170°C fan) / 375F / gas 5.

2. Place the canned apricots and their syrup in a large saucepan, and then add the vanilla and lavender.

3. Bring to a simmer, then pour into a baking dish; add the lime wedges and a pinch of salt before roasting for 25–30 minutes.

4. Remove from the oven and leave to stand for 5 minutes before serving.

Citrus Mint Macaroons

Makes: 16
Preparation time: 40 minutes
Cooking time: 10 minutes
Calories/serving: 181

Ingredients

175 g / 6 oz / 1 ¾ cups ground almonds

350 g / 12 oz / 3 cups icing (confectioners') sugar, sifted

4 medium egg whites

a pinch of salt

175 g / 6 oz / ¾ cup lemon curd

1 tsp lemon extract

a small bunch of mint leaves, picked

Method

1. Preheat the oven to 180°C (160°C fan) / 350F / gas 4. Line two baking trays with greaseproof paper. Combine the ground almonds and 250 g / 9 oz / 2 ½ cups of icing sugar in a bowl.

2. Beat the egg whites in a mixing bowl with a pinch of salt until stiffly peaked. Fold the egg whites into the almond mixture, then spoon into a piping bag.

3. Pipe 32 rounds of the mixture onto the trays. Leave for 15 minutes, then bake for 8–10 minutes, and then remove.

4. Leave to cool. Spread half with lemon curd and sandwich against the other rounds. Mix the remaining icing sugar with the lemon extract and 2 tbsp of hot water to make an icing. Spread the icing and add the mint.

Lemongrass Crème Brûlée

Makes: 4
Preparation time: 5–10 minutes
Cooking time: 55–60 minutes
Calories/serving: 464

Ingredients

4 lemongrass stalks
250 ml / 9 fl. oz / 1 cup whole milk
250 ml / 9 fl. oz / 1 cup double (heavy) cream
6 large egg yolks
125 g / 4 ½ oz / ½ cup caster (superfine) sugar

Method

1. Preheat the oven to 150°C (130°C fan) / 300F / gas 2. Crush 3 of the lemongrass stalks and slice the fourth as a garnish.

2. Combine the milk, cream and crushed lemongrass stalks in a saucepan; bring to a simmer over a moderate heat.

3. Whisk together the egg yolks and sugar in a bowl until pale and thick, then whisk in the milk and cream mixture before straining into a jug.

4. Pour into 4 ramekins and place in a roasting tray; fill the tray with boiling water so that it comes halfway up the sides of the ramekins.

5. Bake in the oven for 45–50 minutes until set and golden and then serve with sliced lemongrass.

Fruit Jellies

Serves: 4
Preparation time: 10–15 minutes
Cooking time: 25 minutes
Calories/serving: 194

Ingredients

250 ml / 9 fl. oz / 1 cup orange juice

9 sheets of gelatine, soaked in cold water

1 large orange, peeled and segmented

300 g / 10 ½ oz / 2 cups strawberries, hulled and chopped

2 tbsp caster (superfine) sugar

350 ml / 12 fl. oz / 1 ½ cups cold water

75 ml / 3 fl. oz / ⅓ cup lemon cordial

1 Conference pear, peeled, cored and sliced

Method

1. Warm the orange juice in a saucepan set over a medium heat. Once simmering, squeeze three sheets of gelatine dry and combine. Stir through the orange segments, then pour into two jars.

2. Purée 250 g / 9 oz / 1 ⅔ cups of the strawberries with the sugar and 100 ml / 3 ½ fl. oz / ½ cup of water in a food processor. Strain into a saucepan.

3. Squeeze dry three sheets of gelatine and whisk into the strawberry liquid. Pour into two jars and chill.

4. Dilute the lemon cordial with the remaining water. Bring to a simmer, then whisk in the remaining gelatine. Fill two jelly moulds with pear slices and strawberries. Top with the lemon liquid and chill until set.

Teacup Chocolate Fondants

Makes: 4
Preparation time:
 10–15 minutes plus chilling
Cooking time: 25 minutes
Calories/serving: 551

Ingredients

2 tbsp butter, melted

2 tbsp caster (superfine) sugar

110 g / 4 oz / ⅔ cup good-quality dark chocolate, chopped

110 g / 4 oz / ½ cup unsalted butter, cubed

2 medium eggs

2 medium egg yolks

75 g / 3 oz / ½ cup gluten-free plain (all-purpose) flour, sifted

Method

1. Preheat the oven to 190°C (170°C fan) / 375F / gas 5. Brush 4 teacups with some of the melted butter before chilling for 15 minutes. Brush with more butter, then dust the insides with sugar and chill again.

2. Melt together the chocolate and cubed butter in a heatproof mixing bowl set over a pan of simmering water.

3. Once melted, remove from the heat. Leave to cool for 5 minutes. Beat together the eggs and egg yolks in a separate mixing bowl until thick.

4. Add the flour to the eggs and whisk until smooth, then fold into the melted chocolate and butter. Spoon into the teacups. Bake for 12–14 minutes until set on top before removing and serving.

Snacks and Treats

If you're trying to lose weight, you need to keep snacks to a minimum, but there's no harm in the occasional treat. Once you change your diet to include more slow-burning, nutrient-rich food, you'll feel fuller for longer, though a healthy snack can still be a good way to keep your energy up throughout the day.

There are lots of options for healthy snacks. A handful of nuts, for example, are packed with protein, so why not keep some handy in your bag or your desk drawer? Veggies dipped in hummus make another great choice.

If you feel the need for something sweet, then use fromage frais as a dip for sliced apples or strawberries. Peanut butter is usually gluten-free, and it goes well with apples or celery. This section has loads of recipes for nutritious gluten-free snacks. Try something new today!

Flapjacks

Serves: 8
Preparation time: 10–15 minutes
Cooking time: 35–40 minutes
Calories/serving: 320

Ingredients

150 g / 5 oz / ⅔ cup unsalted butter, cubed
125 g / 4 ½ oz / ⅓ cup golden syrup
200 g / 7 oz / 2 cups gluten-free oats
100 g / 3 ½ oz / 3 cups cornflakes, crushed
55 g / 2 oz / ⅓ cup raisins
55 g / 2 oz / ⅓ cup dried cranberries
a pinch of salt

Method

1. Preheat the oven to 180°C (160°C fan) / 350F / gas 4. Grease and line a large baking tray with greaseproof paper.

2. Melt the butter and syrup together in a large saucepan until runny. Remove from the heat and stir through the oats, cornflakes, dried fruit and salt.

3. Shape the mixture into patties and arrange, spaced apart, on the tray. Bake for 25–30 minutes until golden brown and set.

4. Remove from the oven and leave to cool before serving.

Mini Raspberry Muffins

Makes: 12
Preparation time: 10 minutes
Cooking time: 15–20 minutes
Calories/serving: 136

Ingredients

110 g / 4 oz / ⅔ cup gluten-free self-raising flour, sifted

½ tsp Xanthan gum

110 g / 4 oz / ½ cup caster (superfine) sugar

110 ml / 4 fl. oz / ½ cup sunflower oil

2 large eggs

1 tsp bicarbonate of (baking) soda

a pinch of salt

55 g / 2 oz / ½ cup shelled pistachios

225 g / 8 oz / 2 cups raspberries

2 tbsp plain yoghurt

Method

1. Preheat the oven to 180°C (160°C fan) / 350F / gas 4 and then line a 12-hole mini muffin tray with paper cases.

2. Combine the flour, Xanthan gum, sugar, oil, eggs, bicarbonate of soda and salt in a large mixing bowl and beat using an electric mixer until just combined.

3. Blitz the pistachios in a food processor until finely ground, then fold into the batter along with the raspberries and yoghurt.

4. Spoon into the muffin cases and bake for 15–20 minutes until risen and a toothpick comes out clean from their centres.

Sweet Lime Popcorn

Serves: 4
Preparation time: 10 minutes
Cooking time: 5 minutes
Calories/serving: 196

Ingredients

3 tbsp sunflower oil

2 limes, zested

75 g / 3 oz / ½ cup popcorn kernels

a pinch of salt

110 g / 4 oz / ½ cup caster (superfine) sugar

Method

1. Heat the oil in a large, heavy-based saucepan set over a moderate heat until hot. Cut the zested limes into wedges.

2. Add the popcorn kernels and a pinch of salt to the hot oil; cover with a lid and cook for 3 minutes, shaking the pan frequently, until the popping stops.

3. Remove from the heat and open carefully; leave to cool slightly.

4. Pulse together the sugar and lime zest until finely ground, then sprinkle over the popcorn and cover with a lid before shaking firmly to coat.

5. Spoon into bowls and serve immediately with lime wedges as a garnish.

Puffed Rice and Chocolate Bars

Serves: 8

Preparation time:
10 minutes plus chilling

Cooking time: 10 minutes

Calories/serving: 296

Ingredients

125 g / 4 ½ oz / 5 cups puffed rice

100 g / 3 ½ oz / 1 cup gluten-free rolled oats

225 g / 8 oz / 1 ½ cups dark chocolate, chopped

2 tbsp golden syrup

55 g / 2 oz / ⅓ cup cocoa powder

75 ml / 3 fl. oz / ⅓ cup semi-skimmed milk

Method

1. Grease and line a 20 cm (8 in) square baking tin with greaseproof paper. Combine the puffed rice and oats in a large mixing bowl, stirring well.

2. Melt together the chocolate and golden syrup in a heatproof bowl set on top of a half-filled saucepan of simmering water.

3. Stir occasionally until the chocolate has melted. Remove from the heat and leave to cool slightly, then add to the rice and oats.

4. Stir well before adding the cocoa powder and milk, then stir thoroughly again.

5. Pack the mixture into the prepared baking tin; cover and chill for 2 hours before turning out and cutting into bars.

Poppy Seed Rounds

Makes: 8
Preparation time: 5–10 minutes
Cooking time: 30 minutes
Calories/serving: 351

Ingredients

110 g / 4 oz / ½ cup unsalted butter
175 g / 6 oz / ¾ cup soft light brown sugar
2 tbsp agave nectar
250 g / 9 oz / 2 ½ cups gluten-free rolled oats
1 tbsp white poppy seeds
55 g / 2 oz / ½ cup black poppy seeds

Method

1. Preheat the oven to 180°C (160°C fan) / 350F / gas 4 and line a large baking tray with greaseproof paper.

2. Melt the butter with the sugar and agave nectar in a large saucepan set over a medium heat; add the oats and stir thoroughly to coat.

3. Stir in the white poppy seeds. Drop scoops of the mixture onto the baking tray, then flatten slightly.

4. Bake for 15–18 minutes until set and golden.

5. Remove to a wire rack to cool; serve with a garnish of black poppy seeds.

Gluten-free Scones

Makes: 12
Preparation time: 10 minutes
Cooking time: 12–15 minutes
Calories/serving: 131

Ingredients

75 g / 3 oz / ⅓ cup butter, cold and cubed

225 g / 8 oz / 1 ½ cups gluten-free
self-raising flour, plus extra for dusting

1 tbsp cornflour (cornstarch)

½ tsp Xanthan gum

½ tsp salt

175 ml / 6 fl. oz / ¾ cup semi-skimmed milk

1 small egg, beaten

Method

1. Preheat the oven to 190°C (170°C fan) / 375F / gas 5. Line a large baking tray with greaseproof paper.

2. Rub the butter into the flour, cornflour, Xanthan gum and salt in a mixing bowl until it resembles breadcrumbs; add the milk and mix well to form a soft dough.

3. Turn out the dough onto a floured surface, pat into a round shape, and roll out to 2 cm (1 in) thickness.

4. Use a 5 cm (2 in) round cutter to stamp out 12 rounds before arranging, spaced apart, on the tray.

5. Brush the tops with beaten egg and bake for 12–15 minutes until golden and risen. Remove to a wire rack to cool completely before serving.

Green Tea Cake

Serves: 8
Preparation time: 10–15 minutes
Cooking time: 45–50 minutes
Calories/serving: 260

Ingredients

100 g / 3 ½ oz / ⅔ cup gluten-free plain (all-purpose) flour

150 g / 5 oz / ⅔ cup margarine, softened

55 g / 2 oz / ½ cup Parmesan, grated

55 g / 2 oz / ⅓ cup brown rice flour

3 small eggs, beaten

2 tbsp cornflour (cornstarch)

1 tsp Xanthan gum

1 tsp salt

110 ml / 4 fl. oz / ½ cup brewed green tea

a large bunch of nettles, roughly chopped

Method

1. Preheat the oven to 180°C (160°C fan) / 350F / gas 4 and line a 900 g (2 lb) loaf tin with greaseproof paper.

2. Combine the flour, margarine, Parmesan, brown rice flour, eggs, cornflour, Xanthan gum and salt in a large mixing bowl, then add the green tea and stir well until thoroughly combined.

3. Add the nettles and stir again briefly to mix. Scrape into the loaf tin.

4. Bake for 45–50 minutes until a cake tester comes out clean from its centre.

5. Remove to a wire rack to cool before turning out, slicing, and serving.

Herbed Apple Chips

Serves: 4
Preparation time: 10 minutes
Cooking time: 50–55 minutes
Calories/serving: 84

Ingredients

4 small Golden Delicious apples, peeled, cored and thinly sliced

2 tbsp sunflower oil

a few sprigs of rosemary, roughly chopped

salt and freshly ground black pepper

Method

1. Preheat the oven to 130°C (110°C fan) / 250F / gas ½ and line a large baking tray with greaseproof paper.

2. Toss the apple slices with the oil, half of the rosemary and some seasoning.

3. Spread out on the baking tray and bake for 50–55 minutes until curled and starting to brown at the edges.

4. Remove from the oven and leave to cool completely before serving with the remaining rosemary as a garnish.

Flourless Chocolate Cake

Serves: 9
Preparation time: 20 minutes
Cooking time: 1 hour 40 minutes
Calories/serving: 557

Ingredients

1 tbsp sunflower oil

300 g / 10 ½ oz / 2 cups dark chocolate, chopped

300 g / 10 ½ oz / 1 ½ cups unsalted butter, cubed

a pinch of salt

5 large eggs

225 g / 8 oz / 1 cup caster (superfine) sugar

Method

1. Preheat the oven to 160°C (140°C fan) / 325F / gas 3 and grease a 20 cm (8 in) square cake tin with sunflower oil.

2. Melt together the chocolate, butter and salt in a heatproof bowl set on top of a half-filled saucepan of simmering water; remove once melted.

3. Beat together the eggs and sugar in a large mixing bowl with an electric whisk until thick and whipped.

4. Fold the melted chocolate into the egg mixture until evenly combined. Pour the batter into the prepared tin and bake for 1 hour 20–30 minutes until the edges start come away from the sides.

5. Remove to a wire rack before cutting and serving.

Cranberry Muffins

Makes: 12
Preparation time: 10 minutes
Cooking time: 15–20 minutes
Calories/serving: 118

Ingredients

110 g / 4 oz / ⅔ cup gluten-free self-raising flour, sifted

½ tsp Xanthan gum

110 g / 4 oz / ½ cup caster (superfine) sugar

110 ml / 4 fl. oz / ½ cup sunflower oil

2 large eggs

1 tsp bicarbonate of (baking) soda

a pinch of salt

55 g / 2 oz / ¼ cup plain yoghurt

150 g / 5 oz / 1 cup dried cranberries

Method

1. Preheat the oven to 180°C (160°C fan) / 350F / gas 4 and line a 12-hole mini muffin tray with paper cases.

2. Combine the flour, Xanthan gum, sugar, oil, eggs, bicarbonate of soda and salt in a large mixing bowl and beat using an electric mixer until just combined; it should still have a few lumps.

3. Add the yoghurt and cranberries and fold into the batter.

4. Spoon into the muffin cases and bake for 15–20 minutes until risen and a toothpick comes out clean from their centres.

5. Leave to cool or serve warm from the oven.

Quinoa Bread

Serves: 6
Preparation time: 25 minutes
Cooking time: 1 hour 25–35 minutes
Calories/serving: 227

Ingredients

200 g / 7 oz / 1 cup quinoa, soaked in
water overnight

100 g / 3 ½ oz / ½ cup millet, soaked in
water overnight

1 tbsp agave nectar

3 tbsp sunflower oil

½ tsp gluten-free baking powder

1 tbsp white wine vinegar

2 tbsp cornflour (cornstarch)

250 ml / 9 fl. oz / 1 cup water

1 tbsp sesame seeds, to garnish

salt and freshly ground black pepper

Method

1. Drain the quinoa and millet and spread out
on a large tray lined with kitchen paper;
leave to dry for 10 minutes.

2. Preheat the oven to 160°C (140°C fan) /
325F / gas 3. Line a 900 g (2 lb) loaf tin with
greaseproof paper.

3. Combine the grains with the remaining
ingredients apart from the sesame seeds;
process for 2–3 minutes until a sticky batter
comes together.

4. Scrape the batter into the loaf tin and
bake for 1 hour 25–35 minutes until golden
and risen. Pierce the loaf with a knife after
45 minutes.

5. Turn out and cut into slices before serving
with a garnish of sesame seeds.

Chestnut Prune Cookies

Makes: 16
Preparation time: 20 minutes
Cooking time: 10–12 minutes
Calories/serving: 176

Ingredients

150 g / 5 oz / ⅔ cup unsalted butter, softened

75 g / 3 oz / ⅓ cup caster (superfine) sugar

½ tsp vanilla extract

110 g / 4 oz / ⅔ cup dried prunes, soaked in hot water

4 medium egg yolks

150 g / 5 oz / 1 cup chestnut flour

100 g / 3 ½ oz / ⅔ cup gluten-free plain (all-purpose) flour, plus extra for dusting

½ tsp gluten-free baking powder

a pinch of salt

Method

1. Preheat the oven to 180°C (160°C fan) / 350F / gas 4 and line a large baking tray with greaseproof paper.

2. Cream together the butter, sugar, and vanilla extract in a large mixing bowl until pale and thick.

3. Pulse together the prunes with some of the soaking liquid and egg yolks; add to the creamed butter and mix well.

4. Add the flours, baking powder and salt, stirring well until a dough forms, then turn out onto a floured surface and knead briefly.

5. Roll out to ½ cm (¼ in) thickness and use a cookie cutter to stamp out rounds; arrange on the tray and bake for 10–12 minutes before removing to a wire rack to cool.

Meal Plans and Diary

When starting a new diet, it's important to have a plan. Otherwise you'll have a day – probably fairly early on where you're pressed for time and don't have a gluten-free menu planned or ingredients bought. It's at times like these that you're likely to reach for whatever is available... which may contain gluten.

Before you start, sit down and think about how you want to tackle going gluten-free. If you've been diagnosed with coeliac disease, follow your doctor's or dietitian's advice. If not, do you want to go cold turkey, or cut gluten out of your diet more gradually? Maybe you could start by eating one gluten-free meal a day for the first week, then two in the second and so on. Also, jot down some targets for exercise and weight loss. It may seem like a lot to think about, but once you get into the swing of things it will all become second nature.

Have a go

In this chapter, you can plan and track your progress for four weeks. You can mix and match the recipes in this book, or search out new ones. What's included here is only the tip of the iceberg as far as delicious gluten-free food is concerned!

Once you've got your plan in place and your shopping list written, make sure you keep a record of everything you eat and drink. In addition, jot down how you feel and any digestive symptoms that you may have. If you're still having symptoms after going fully gluten-free, it may be something else that's causing them. Your food diary can help you and your GP look for a pattern and find a solution.

Week 1

	Breakfast	Lunch	Snack	Dinner
Monday				
Tuesday				
Wednesday				
Thursday				
Friday				
Saturday				
Sunday				

New foods that I've tried

Exercise log

Starting and finishing weight

How I feel

Week 2

	Breakfast	Lunch	Snack	Dinner
Monday				
Tuesday				
Wednesday				
Thursday				
Friday				
Saturday				
Sunday				

New foods that I've tried

Exercise log

Starting and finishing weight

How I feel

Week 3

	Breakfast	Lunch	Snack	Dinner
Monday				
Tuesday				
Wednesday				
Thursday				
Friday				
Saturday				
Sunday				

New foods that I've tried

Exercise log

Starting and finishing weight

How I feel

Week 4

	Breakfast	Lunch	Snack	Dinner
Monday				
Tuesday				
Wednesday				
Thursday				
Friday				
Saturday				
Sunday				

New foods that I've tried

Exercise log

Starting and finishing weight

How I feel

A Gluten-free Kitchen

It's easiest to stick to a gluten-free diet if your kitchen cupboards aren't full of wheat-based foods. Before you start, have a clear-out and get rid of the things you're no longer going to eat. Stocking your cupboards with a range of gluten-free ingredients and foods is the first step towards a healthier new you!

Here are some of the basic ingredients that no gluten-free kitchen should be without:

Grains and pulses

buckwheat

brown rice

chickpeas (garbanzo beans)

corn tortillas (check the label)

gluten-free oats

kidney beans

lentils

quinoa

Gluten-free flours

almond flour (or ground almonds)

brown rice flour

cornflour (cornstarch)

gluten-free flour blends

hazelnut (cobnut) flour

millet flour

oat flour (check the label)

potato flour

quinoa flour

soy flour

Cooking essentials

dried herbs

olive oil

mustard

pasta sauce (check the label)

salt and pepper

spices

stock cubes (many are gluten-free)

tinned fruit

tinned vegetables

vegetable oil

vegetable stock

vinegar

Snacks

dried fruit

nuts (check for cross contamination warnings)

popcorn

pumpkin seeds

rice cakes

sunflower seeds

vegetable crisps

Once your store cupboard is stocked, you can buy the perishable ingredients that you'll need to cook your gluten-free meals. Many of these foods are naturally gluten-free, and there are plenty to choose from! This list is just a start:

Vegetables

asparagus

beansprouts

broccoli

carrots

curly kale

onions

peppers

potatoes

spinach

squash

sweet potatoes

Fruits

apples

bananas

berries

citrus fruit

mangoes

pears

Meat and protein

bacon

beef

chicken

eggs

fish

lamb

pork

shellfish

Milk and dairy

cheese (check the label on shredded cheese)

milk

sour cream

yoghurt (check the label)

If you're on a budget, plan ahead and make use of your freezer. You can make big batches of dishes such as bolognese sauce and freeze the leftovers. You can also make use of multi-buy offers on meat, and freeze what you don't need straightaway.

Keep it fresh

One downside to gluten-free food substitutes, such as bread, is that they usually don't contain the preservatives used in regular bread. This means that they can dry out more quickly, so you need to store them properly. Once opened, keep them in an airtight container in a dark, dry place. You can refrigerate them to make them last a bit longer, and you can even keep your bread in the freezer.

Keeping it Off

Congratulations – you've done it! You've stuck to the gluten-free diet and are feeling the benefits already. You've got more energy, you feel great and you've lost some weight.

Now comes the next challenge: keeping it off. Many dieters reach their target and then lose the motivation to stick with the new routine, putting the weight straight back on again. It doesn't have to happen to you. Here are a few tips for keeping motivated:

- Remember why you did it! Have a look at an old photo of yourself, or look back at your food diary. Think about how you felt before cutting out gluten, and focus on how much better you're feeling – and looking – now.

- Set a new target. For example, now that you're healthier and fitter, maybe you could train for a fun run, or even a half marathon. Keeping focused on goals can help stop you from backtracking.

- Don't get stuck in a rut. Set yourself the goal of trying two or three new gluten-free recipes every week.

- If you've gone down a size, clear out some of your old clothes, and treat yourself to a few things in your new size.

- Keep track. If you have a target weight, weigh yourself once a week to help you stay on track.

- Set an example. Your friends and family will notice how much better you're looking and feeling. Helping someone else to go gluten-free can keep you motivated to stick with it yourself.

The important thing is not to see a gluten-free diet as a 'quick fix'. It's a long-term lifestyle change that should leave you happier, fitter and healthier. Before long, you won't even miss the foods you've eliminated!

Diet consultant: Jo Stimpson.

Written by: Ruth Manning.

Main food photography and recipe development: PhotoCuisine UK.

Picture Credits

All photos by Photo Cuisine except: Dreamstime: 7 Lanak, 9 Antikainen, 13 Syda Productions, 17 Mariemilyphotos, 18 Murdock2013, 21 Hpphoto, 22 Lucidwaters, 24 Photographerlondon, 26 Photoeuphoria, 27 Steve Allen, 28 Dmitri Maruta, 31 Diego Vito Cervo, 32 Antoni Halim, 37b, 86b Jf123, 39b, 125t Mohamed Osama; 42b wabeno, 43b Alexstar, 44b Valentyn75, 45b Tamara Kulikova, 46b Anitasstudio, 47b, 79b Pongphan Ruengchai, 48b, 115 Ovydyborets, 52b Olga Lupol, 57b Kirill Krasnov, 58b Elovich, 61b Oksix, 65b Svetlana Kuznetsova, 69b Zts, 72b Mariusz Blach, 74b Irochka, 75b Lockstockbob, 76b, 116 Blackroom, 77b Gresei, 81b Natika, 83b Eyewave, 87b Norgal, 88b Serhiy Shullye, 92b Roman Samokhin, 93b, 119 Olga Lupol, 94b Blankstock, 102b Sommai Sommai, 104b Ruslan Grigolava, 105b Robyn Mackenzie, 110b Leerodney Avison, 112 Andres Rodriguez, 122 Sarahgen, 126 Hongqi Zhang (aka Michael Zhang), 127 Mjth; Shutterstock: 4 Andresr, 6 pieropoma, 8 iko, 10 Phil Date, 11 Elena Elisseeva, 12 Syda Productions, 14 Anna Hoychuk, 15 Hong Vo, 16 Brent Hofacker, 19 Richard M Lee, 20 Monkey Business Images, 23 Yulia von Eisenstein, 25 lithian, 29 Pressmaster, 30 Monkey Business Images, 33 Olesia Bilkei, 36b M. Unal Ozmen, 38b EM Arts, 40b, 114 Tim UR, 41b, 71b, 125 Nattika, 49b Vova Shevchuk, 53b Christian Jung, 54b, 120 Alex459, 55b Binh Thanh Bui, 56b Antonio S, 59b, 117 Arunas Gabalis, 60b topseller, 62b, 100b, 118 M. Unal Ozmen, 63b Kazlouski Siarhei, 64b NIPAPORN PANYACHAROEN, 68b turtix, 70b Nuttapong, 73b Teresa Azevedo, 78b Egor Rodynchenko, 80b Davydenko Yuliia, 82b Iryna Denysova, 89b, 97b, 103b, 108b Picsfive, 90b homydesign, 91b ppi09, 95b Volha Kuznetsova, 96b, 121 Maks Narodenko, 101b Sailorr, 106b Scisetti Alfio, 107b Volosina, 109b Dionisvera, 111b Volosina, 113 ElenaGaak, 123 maradonna 8888, 124 Alexander Tihonov, 128 wavebreakmedia.